COLLECTORS GU

Tonka® Trucks

1947-1963

By Don & Barb DeSalle

Published by L-W Book Sales, P.O. Box 69, Gas City, IN 46933

ISBN #: 0-89538-055-2

Table of Contents

PREFACE

Tonka has been a part of American history for almost half a century. Tonka trucks have demonstrated strong market value for half a decade, as the values of mint conditioned Tonka continues to soar. The beauty of collecting Tonka is the number and variety of trucks produced. While some pressed steel series can be completed with twenty to forty trucks, the advanced Tonka collection will contain hundreds of trucks. The purpose of the *"Collectors Guide to Tonka Trucks 1947-1963"* , is to provide a quality reference book on Tonka Trucks produced from 1947 through 1963, including some more desirable trucks and collectible items from later years.

The objectives of this book are: First, to show the examples of Tonka trucks in quality full color photographs. Color photographs are more descriptive than words, and we were fortunate the publisher felt all color photographs were essential to the quality of the book. Second, is to provide a history of the Tonka Corporation from its earliest development through its current status in the Hasbro, Corporation. The third objective is to provide identification to differentiate the production years of Tonka trucks from 1947 through 1963. The fourth objective is to divide the book into sections that describe the type of truck, rather than the production year. The structure of the book is designed to easily identify trucks by categorizing them into twelve descriptive groupings. The correct Tonka stock numbers are used for each truck. Also included, is a miscellaneous section for trucks and accessories that do not fit into the major groupings of Tonka trucks within this book. The fifth purpose is to provide a current price guide reflective of today's market. The price guide includes good, excellent, and mint prices and reflects the average "real money" value across the country. Note: Mint, boxed trucks can command twenty to fifty percent increase in the highest price value listed. Prices will vary slightly according to the region of the country and to the economics of the region.

The authors are considered the leading collectors of Tonka in the United States. Don and Barb DeSalle are always seeking to buy excellent to mint, Tonka trucks and private labeled trucks. This book will serve as a guide to the advanced as well as the novice collector. Please call Don or Barb at 1-800-392-Toys for comments on the information contained in this book, or Tonka trucks available for sale.

HISTORY

In 1946, in the basement of a small schoolhouse in Mound, Minnesota, Lynn E. Baker, Avery Crounse and Alvin Tesch founded Mound Metalcraft Co. The company was incorporated September 18, 1946. The primary production was a major output of hoes, rakes and shovels, along with tie, hat and shoe racks. Toy production was a sideline. During the first year, the company purchased tooling from the L.E. Streeter Co. for a toy Steam Shovel. Tooling was refined, and Mound produced their first two toys, a Steam Shovel and Crane. After a successful debut at the New York Toy Show in 1946, Mound Metalcraft manufactured a total of 37,000 pieces of the two metal toys, the #100 Steam Shovel and the #150 Crane and Clam. Tonka Toys, named after Lake Minnetonka, enjoyed the first of what would be many years of successful sales in the toy truck business. A resident of Mound, Minnesota, Erling W. Eklof, was asked to design the first Tonka logo. In three days, the logo was designed to represent the lake area in which the plant was located. The waves reflected the waters of Lake Minnetonka. Eklof added three birds and a distinctive swash type of lettering. This logo would remain unchanged from 1947 until 1955. This first Tonka catalog was printed in 1949.

The founding premise of Tonka trucks was to provide consumers with a toy that was durable, reasonably priced, and of course, FUN! Tonka devoted much time and resource designing and testing each Tonka truck. Three decades after its initial founding, the company grew from the original small schoolhouse with a half dozen employees, to an expansive plant covering nearly 1/3 mile along the shore of Lake Minnetonka employing over 1,300 people that produced approximately 400,000 toys per week. The initial two toys produced increased to 125 toys during the following three decades.

The production of Tonka Toys followed many of the same techniques used in the mass production of trucks and cars in the auto capitol, Detroit, Michigan. Tonka's design procedures closely paralleled those used by Detroit's major auto makers. A new toy began as a sketch, and was then tested with consumers. If a sketch received favorable reviews, the toy was then translated into a three dimensional form of clay by model builders.

Clay models that received a favorable reaction were formed into metal or fiberglass. These models were then reviewed by people involved with child supervision, and early childhood development. If the toy passed the inspection of this group, a detailed engineering drawing and blueprints were prepared and manufacturing specifications were developed. When trial production samples were completed, they were sent out for the toughest test of all – the **children!**

Tonka's production and management staff watched the reaction of children as they played with the toys. Tonka confirmed the toy's play value, how well interest was retained, and safety and durability. If the toy passed the final tests, Tonka mass produced and marketed the toy.

Since the initial production in 1947, Tonka has become a world-wide operation. Late in 1955, Mound Metalcraft changed its name to Tonka Toys, Inc. In 1991, Tonka became part of Hasbro, Inc., and Tonka trucks continue to be the #1 brand in the non-powered truck category. Each year Hasbro introduces a dynamic line of fun, innovative, state of the art trucks for children of all ages.

ABOUT THE AUTHORS

Don DeSalle and his wife Barb are nationally known authorities and collectors of Tonka Trucks. The DeSalles are licensed by Hasbro, Inc. to write the book titled *"Collector's Guide to Tonka Trucks 1947-1963"*. The DeSalles have traveled many miles coast to coast to pursue Tonka Trucks, both as collectors and dealers. Through the knowledge they have acquired at the antique toy shows they promote, as well as attend, the DeSalles have an excellent knowledge base for the market value of Tonka Trucks. Don and Barb DeSalle are always buying excellent to mint Tonka Trucks and private labeled Tonkas. 1-800-392-TOYS.

The trucks and miscellaneous items featured in this book are from Don and Barb DeSalle's private collection. Through a team effort, the DeSalles have acquired one of the most outstanding Tonka Truck collections in the country. The DeSalles are also licensed to reproduce replacement parts for antique Tonka Trucks. Those reproduction replacement parts are available through Julian Thomas, Thomas Toy Parts, Fenton, MI. (810) 629-8707.

Don DeSalle, a native of Toledo, Ohio, graduated from Rogers High School. Don was all state in football, and received a scholarship to play football for Indiana University. Don went on to obtain a B.A. (70) and M.A. (72) from Indiana University in Geology and Chemistry, and was named an All American football player, playing in the Rose Bowl, the Senior Bowl, and the North and South game. His football career continued as he played briefly with the Buffalo Bills.

Don taught high school science and coached football for several years. His interest in race cars lead to his ownership of Paragon Speedway, a sprint car track. Currently, Don is one of the largest antique toy show promoters in the United States. In the near future, he will be manufacturing the DeSalle line of limited edition trucks.

Barb DeSalle, a native of Daleville, IN, obtained a B.S. (71), M.S. (75), Ed. S. (81). She has completed the coursework on her doctorate, and is doing research on Satellite Communications, at Ball State University. Barb is past president of Anderson University Phi Delta Kappa, and has served as a middle school principal, high school assistant principal, dean of girls, grant proposal development director, and a teacher. Barb and Don are constantly busy with DeSalle Promotions, Inc., promoting antique toy shows across the country.

The DeSalles have three children, Dan and Chris DeSalle, and Sonja Gentry. Dan and Sonja are students at Indiana University, and Chris is in high school. All three help with the toy shows as their schedules allow.

TONKA LOGOS

1947 – 1955

1970 – 1973

1956 – 1957

1974 – 1975

1958 – 1961

1976 – 1977

1962 – 1969

1978 – Present

IDENTIFICATION

The first two toys produced by Mound Metalcraft in 1947 were the #100 Steam Shovel and the #150 Crane and Clam. The shovel, crane and clam were very simple toys, with hard rubber wheels. In 1949 rubber tracks were added to these toys. Another early toy introduced by Mound Metalcraft in 1948 was the #200 Power Lift Truck and Trailer. 1949 was the introduction of the #190 Loading Tractor. The first toy trucks introduced in 1949, bore a slight resemblance to the F-6 Ford Cabover Trucks of that era.

The cabover, or snub nose trucks were all designed the same except for the grilles and tires. The 1949 – 1952 cabs had three even, horizontal and parallel lines or stampings, all approximately 2 1/2 inches long, simulating a grille. In 1953, the lines of the grille were changed. The top line was approximately 7/8 inches long, and the bottom line approximately 2 inches long. The wheels of the cabover or snub nosed trucks were assembled from two stamped steel pieces, held together by a brass bushing, and had thin rubber tires. The 1953, cab over truck tires carried the logo "Tonka Toys . . . . Made in U.S.A." on the sidewalls.

Tonka introduced its new restyled trucks in 1954 called "Round Fendered" by collectors. These trucks were made with a conventional cab and the engines were out front and resembled the F100-Fords. This particular cab style would be used by Tonka through 1957. Another change incorporated into the entire truck line was the use of rubber tires and a hub cap which had simulated lug bolts and had five round holes stamped in them.

Two grille designs were used during this period 1954-1957. Trucks from the years 1954-1955 were made with a grille that was part of the bumper. The grille and bumper were attached by two tabs at the bottom of the bumper and held secure by two metal snap-in head lights.

In 1956-57, the bumper was separate from the grille held in place by two rivets. The grille was held in place by two plastic lights. Lights prior to this were metal. Another feature of the 1957 trucks were the window pillars, which now came straight down and not at an angle as on previous years trucks. In general, 1957 trucks were very similar to the '56 trucks, with the exception of a hood scoop in the middle of the hood, and the previously mentioned window pillars. Mud flaps appeared in 1955 and were used on various trucks until 1957. Dump trucks, semis, boxed vans and long wheel base trucks carried mud flaps.

In 1958 Tonka introduced their new designed cabs called "Square Fender" trucks by collectors which would be used through 1961 with slight modifications. This design represented the new 1957 Ford Cabs in the F series line. The grille now carried dual headlights and had a "T" stamped in the middle of it. 1958 also saw the beginning of plastic windshields. 1958-59 trucks carried 4 parallel ridges on the hood. 1958 hub caps were the same as the 54-57 trucks with 5 round holes. Bumpers were thicker with two tow hooks. In 1959, white walls were introduced, and either solid disc or five triangular holes in the hub caps. 1960 saw a slight hood change, the center two ridges were no longer parallel, but were placed at slight angles converging at the front of the hood. This also was similar to styling changes made by Ford. Tonka's trucks of 1961 were similar to those of 1960 except that the "T" was removed from the grille and placed in the center of the newly designed bumper.

The trucks after 1961 known as "generic trucks" by collectors marked the end of the Tonka trucks resembling the F series Fords. Many Tonka collectors concentrate on particular series of Tonka trucks. ie. Cabovers, Round Fenders, or Square Fenders. Today the Generic Trucks are becoming more popular. They are being sought out by collectors, and will gain their place in the collection of trucks.

1947-48 Tonka Toys Decal.

7

1949-52 Cabover cab has three parallel horizontal lines to simulate grille.

1953 Cabover cab, three lines in grille are different sizes, tires are embossed with "Tonka Toys . . . Made in U.S.A. on side walls.

1949-1953 Cabover Tonka Decal.

1954-55 Mound Metalcraft, Inc.
Tonka Toys Decal.

1956-57 Tonka Toys Decal
Mound Metalcraft, Inc.
was dropped from decals.

1958-1961 Tonka Toys Decal.

1962-1964 Tonka Toys Decal.

1955
One piece grille and bumper,
hubcaps have five round holes,
large slanted windshield posts.

1956
Separate grille held in place
with plastic lights.
Five round holes in hub caps,
large slanted windshield posts.

1957 – Air scoop on hood.
Snap in plastic lights hold grille
in place. Five round holes in
hub caps. Windshield posts
vertical and thinner.

1958
Four even spaced bars in hood,
"T" in grille. Five round holes
in hub caps.

1959
Four even spaced bars on hood,
"T" in grille. Five triangular shaped
holes in the hub caps.

1960
"V" in the center of hood, "T" in grille.

"V" in the center of hood.
No "T" in grille.
"T" now in new bumper style.

1962-63
One piece grille and bumper,
referred to as "Generic Trucks"
as they don't resemble any
particular truck.

"Generic" truck grille is changed,
one light on each side.
Windows on all four sides of cab.

CABOVER TRUCKS

The first Tonka toys were manufactured in 1947. The #100 Steam Shovel had a red cab and the #150 Crane and Clam had a yellow cab. Both toys had four rubber tires. A total of 37,000 of these two toys were produced in 1947. A new product was added in 1948, the #200 Lift Truck and Cart. The early examples of this unique toy were made of aluminum.

In 1949, Tonka first introduced the cabover or snub nose cab trucks. These toy trucks represented the actual F-6 Ford Trucks of the same period. The cabs had a simple plated bumper riveted to the cab, and three evenly spaced and length stampings representing the grille. Tires were made of rubber with three ridges that resembled treads and were mounted on steel rims with brass bushings. Minor changes were made to the cab and tires in 1953. The three grille lines or stampings were no longer even in length and the tires carried the words "Tonka Toys . . . made in the U.S.A.", on the sidewalls.

Tonka introduced four trucks in 1949, the #130 Tractor – Carry-All, the #140 Tonka Toy Transport, the #180 Dump Truck, and the #250 Wrecker Truck. The rubber tires on the #150 Crane and Clam were replaced with rubber crawler tracks on steel wheels. A rare item for 1949 was the #300 Doll Hospital Bed and Mattress. This was dropped in 1950 and replaced with the #310 Doll Bed!

In 1950, Tonka introduced three new trucks, the #145 Steel Carrier with an orange cab, the #185 Tonka Express Truck, and the #175 Utility Truck. 1951 saw the introduction of the first "Allied" semi truck. Tonka enjoyed a long association with "Allied" for over 30 years. During this 30 year period, various forms of "Allied" trucks were produced.

Two new trucks were introduced in 1952, the #500 Live Stock Hauler, and the #550 Grain Hauler. In 1952, Tonka also replaced the steel bottom of the #140 Tonka Toy Transporter with wood instead of steel, and the rear piano hinged doors were replaced with a new friction type door that had two plated handles.

In 1953, three new toys were introduced, the #600-3 Road Grader, the style of which remained very similar through 1965, the #650-3 "Green Giant" transport, and the #575-3 "Tonka Logger". The first of many sets were introduced by Tonka in 1953. The #675-3 "Tonka" Trailer Fleet was manufactured. This fleet consisted of one red cab, one blue cab, the #130-3 Carry-All Trailer, the #500-3 Live Stock Trailer, the #550 Grain Hauler, the #575-3 "Tonka" Logger Trailer, and the #650-3 Green Giant Trailer.

The rarest truck in the cabover production was the #185 Tonka Express Truck, produced only in 1950. This truck was a box truck, the cab and chassis was red, the box was green, and the truck had duel rear wheels. The sides of the box carried a large white "Tonka Express" decal with equally large "Tonka" logo. This will be a tough truck to find for your Tonka Cabover collection.

1949 Carry-All Trailer #170
came with #150 Crane & Clam.
This is the only year it
came in yellow and green.
#130 Carry-All.

1947 Steam Shovel #100.

1947 Crane and clam #150.

1949 Crane and clam
with tracks #150

1948 Powerlift Truck and Trailer #200.

1949 Steam Shovel #50.

1949 Steam Shovel #100 with tracks.

1953 Steam Shovel #50.

1953 Road Grader #600

1953 Wrecker Truck #250
made from 1949-53.

Dump Truck #180,
1949-53.

1950 Tonka Express #185
(very rare)

1953 Green Giant Utility Truck
Has solid rubber tires, as
used in later years.

Utility Truck #175.
1950-51 Green Cab / Yellow Body
1952-53 Orange Cab / Green Body.

1953 Utility Truck #175-3

18

1952 Coast to Coast
Utility Truck.

1952-53 Livestock Van #500.

1952-53 Grain Hauler #550.

1953 Log Hauler #575.

1950-1953 Steel Carrier #145.
Cab comes in both orange
and yellow colors.

1953 Flatbed Semi.

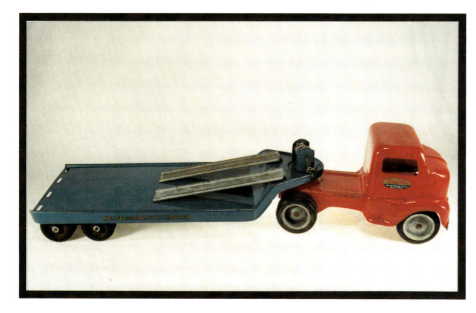

1949-50 Tractor and Carry-All #120.

1953 Tractor and Carry-All #130.
Offered alone without shovel in 1949.

1953 Allied Van Lines #400.

1953 Green Giant Transport #650.

1949 Tonka Toy Transport #140.
Hinged doors, silver roof.

1950-52 Tonka Toy Transport
#140, with red roof.

Ace Tractor and Trailer.

1952 Marshall Field and Company.

1953 Meier and Frank Semi.

1953 Wilson Semi.

1953 Our Own Hardware.
(single axle)

1953 Our Own Hardware.
(dual axle)

1953 G. Fox and Company Semi.

BOX VANS

The first Tonka Box Van was produced in 1950, the #185 Tonka Express Truck. This truck had a red cab and chassis, with a green box. The van had no rear doors, but instead had a functional end gate.

The next Tonka Box Van was in 1954, the #725-4 Star-Kist Van. The colors of the van were a red cab and chassis and a dark blue van body. The van body had dual rear wheels, wood floors, and two friction rear doors with fluted handles. Approximately 20,000 of the Star-Kist Vans were made.

The #750-5 Minute-Maid Van was introduced in 1955. The entire truck was white. The same type box as the Star-Kist was used with dual rear wheels and mud flaps. In 1956 the Minute Maid body was lowered on the chassis and the wood floor was replaced with steel. The dual rear wheels also gave way to a single wheel on each side.

The #01 Tonka Service Van was introduced in 1959, and again in 1960. It was painted a medium metallic blue, and carried an 8 1/2 inch aluminum ladder mounted in brackets below the roof. No rear doors were used, and benches were added to seat the make-believe workers.

Another unique toy from Tonka in 1959 was the #36 Tandem Air Express. Similar to the earlier Minute Maid Box Van, the Tandem Air Express had metal floors and rear doors. This truck also carried a pup. The pup was a box van mounted on four wheels with a steerable front bracket and hitch.

The #105 Rescue Squad truck was introduced in 1960. It was the same box truck as the #01 1959 Tonka Service Van. The Rescue Squad truck was all white, with a flasher on the cab roof, a siren on the left front fender, an 8 1/2 inch white ladder mounted inside, and a red plastic boat on the roof. The #105 Rescue Squad truck was also part of the 1960 #225 Fire Department set.

A number of private label box trucks were made over the years. The trucks known to exist are as follows: 1954 Hardware Hank, 1954 True Value, 1956 Robin Hood Flour, 1956 Bruce Floor Wax, and the 1959 Terminix Van.

1950 Express Truck #185.
(Very Rare)

1954 Star-Kist Box Van #725.

1955 Minute Maid Box Van.
Note: Duel rear wheels and higher
box than on #56 Box Trucks.

1956 Minute Maid Box Van.

1954 True Value Box Van.

1954 Hardware Hank Box Van.

1955 Bruce Floor Wax Box Van.
(Rare)

1956 Robin Hood Flour Box Van.
(Rare)

1959 Terminix Van.

1961 Terminix Van.

1959 Tonka Air Express #16.

1959 Tonka Air Express
with pup #36.

1959-61 Tonka Service Van.

1961 Tonka Service Van #103.

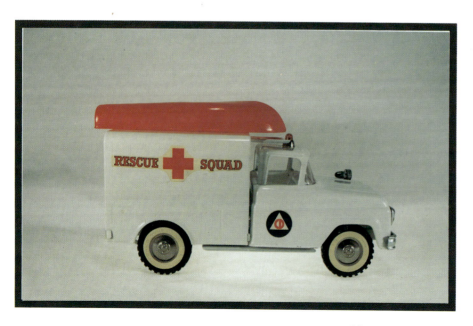

1960-61 Rescue Van #105.

DUMP TRUCKS

Tonka first produced the #180 Dump Truck in 1949. The red and green Cabover Dump Truck was manufactured from 1949–1953. Only the 1949 models carried a #180 on the side of the dump beds. 1954 saw the introduction of the "Round Fender" version of the red and green Dump Truck. The #180-4 had a new redesigned dump box, with four ribs and was riveted to the chassis.

Hi-Way Dump Trucks appeared in 1956 with the Dump Truck in Omaha orange. New in the Dump Truck line was the #980-6 Hydraulic Side Dump. This was Tonka's first hydraulic operated toy using the aluminum hydraulic cylinder to dump the bed of the truck. This truck had two sides that would open and a tail gate that would open by tripping the side lever. New for 1957 was the 3-in-1 Hi-Way Service Truck, which was a hydraulic side dump packaged with a "V" plow and a scraper blade. These two accessories made the dumps look very attractive. Produced in 1957, was one of the most sought after Hi-Way Trucks ever made by Tonka, the #45 "Big Mike". The "Big Mike" was named after the grandson of one of Tonka's founders, Lynn E. Baker. This was the biggest and heaviest Dump Truck in the Tonka Toy line, weighing 6 3/4 pounds. Twin hydraulic rams lifted the large load that the dump bed would carry. The 1957 "Big Mike" or the 1958 "Square Fender" version are much sought after by Tonka collectors.

The #42 "Land Rover" described by many as the most unusual dump truck manufactured by Tonka, was produced in 1959. The "Land Rover" was basically a "Big Mike" with a new style of tires. The tires are 2 3/8 inches wide, resembling skate board wheels. Many early collectors found the trucks and removed the wheels replacing them with the original type rubber tires, assuming someone had changed the tires from the original "Big Mike" tires. There were not many of the "Land Rovers" produced and are an excellent find for the Tonka collector.

1949-1953 Cabover
Dump Truck.

1955 Aerial Sand Loader Set.

1956 Aerial Sand Loader Set
#825-6

1955 Dump Truck,
made 1955-1957.

1957 Hydraulic Dump Truck.

1956 Hi-Way Dump Truck.

1957 Side Dump.

1957 Big Mike
Dual Dump Truck, hydraulic.

1959 Hi-Way Dump Truck.

1959 Hi-Way Side Dump.

1958 Big Mike
Dual Hydraulic.

1959 Land Rover
Hydraulic Dump Truck.
Note: Large flotation type
tires on rover.

1958 Dump Truck.

1960 Hydraulic Dump Truck.

1961 Dump Truck and Sandloader
#116

1961 Hydraulic Dump Truck.

1961 Grading Service #134

1962 Dump Truck with Sand Loader
#616

1962 Hydraulic Dump Truck
#520

FIRE TRUCKS

In 1954 Tonka introduced the #700-4 Aerial Ladder Truck. The first trucks carried the decal "M – F – D", referring to Mound Fire Department. This truck came with two scaling ladders and four fire extinguishers and a ladder which could be raised by turning a hand wheel. The 1954 Ladder Truck had no fancy scrolling and no red light, only a cast siren on the roof, and a #5 on the door and rear seat. In 1956 the #700-6 Ladder Truck carried the "T – F – D" decals and a cast siren was mounted on the left fender, with a tapered flasher with a red lens on the roof. Scroll work was still on gas tanks and a "T F D" on the side of the hood.

1956 also saw the introduction of the #950-6 Suburban Pumper. These trucks first had threaded fittings and a hand grab bar across the back. Later trucks came without a grab bar and the threaded hoses were eliminated for a much simpler friction type fitting. These fittings will remain throughout the duration of pumpers in years to come. Also introduced in 1956, was a cast fire hydrant that acted as a reducer from the garden hose. The hydrant reduced water pressure so you could actually put out pretend fires using the reel of booster hose mounted on top of the truck bed. Fire trucks could be purchased separately or in a complete set, the #900-6 which included the Aerial Ladder Truck, the Suburban Pumper, and a white Rescue Squad Van. In 1958, the Rescue Van was replaced with the white T.F.D. Tanker and in 59, only the two items, the pumper and ladder, were boxed together. This incidentally, was the only year the trucks were made in white.

1954 Ladder Truck
Note: Two extra ladders & M-F-D decals #700.

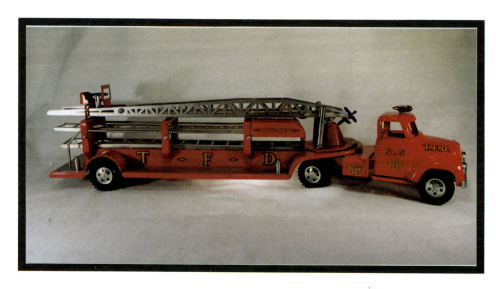

1956 Aerial Ladder #700-6.

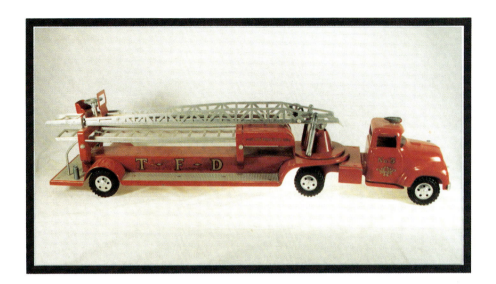

1957 Hydraulic Aerial Ladder
Truck #48.

1958 Aerial Ladder
Truck #48.

1959 Ladder Truck
(white, only this year)
came with #B212 set.

1962 Aerial Ladder Truck
#1348.

1956-57 Fire Department Rescue Van
comes with pumper and ladder
set #B212.

1958 T.F.D. Tanker
came with red pumper and ladder
set #3212.

1956 Suburban Pumper #46
Grab bar on back.
Early models had threaded
hose fittings.

1957 Suburban Pumper #46.

1958 Suburban Pumper #46.

1959 Suburban Pumper
(white, only this year)
part of #B212
2 piece fire set of 1959.

1960 Suburban Pumper #926.

1963 Suburban Pumper #926
side doors are no longer functional.

Rescue Squad Van
This was first introduced as part of the 1959
red #B225 three piece fire set.

1963-64 Fire Jeep #425.

HI-WAY TRUCKS

The most popular trucks with collectors, in the Tonka line, are the Hi-Way Trucks, first introduced in 1956. The 1956 models were the Pickup Truck, Side Dump Truck, Dump Truck, and Hi-Way Grader when purchased in the #975-6 set. Eight hi-way signs were included. Tonka made the set again in 1957, the #B208 "Hi-Way Department" set. New for 1957 was the #42 "Big Mike", the #40 Shovel and Carry-All Trailer, and the addition of "V" Plows and Scraper Plows. A very desirable set in 1957 was the B210 Road Building set. Included in this set was the "Big Mike", the Carry-All and Shovel, Dump Truck, and Grader.

Along with the regular Omaha orange used on Hi-Way Trucks, Tonka introduced a new color, lime or euclid green for 1958. These trucks could only be purchased in the #B207 Hi-Way Construction Set. The set included the Carry-All and Steam Shovel, Dump Truck with Scraper Plow, and a Grader. In 1959, the steam shovel was replaced with the #44 euclid green Dragline and the Scraper Plow was deleted. Tonka would manufacture this set again in 1960. Another unique truck manufactured in 1960 was the #125 euclid green Low Boy and Dozer. The Dozer was similar to the #100 orange Dozer, the Low Boy included tow aluminum Loading Ramps, and the cab carried only the Tonka logo on its side. Due to the limited production of this set, only one year, this makes a great addition to your Tonka collection.

The #135 Mobile Dragline was also new for 1960. The Dragline was mounted on a new flat-bed truck and chassis and was painted entirely Omaha orange, except for the Boom and Dragline in black. The Dragline was also in the #B220 State Turnpike set. This set included the Dragline, Pickup, Dump Truck, and #100 Dozer, two Road Signs and a Road Barrier. The Mobile Dragline was manufactured only one year and it is difficult to find excellent examples for your Tonka collection. The #118 Giant Dozer was introduced in 1961 along with the #142 Mobile Clam. The Mobile Clam was basically identical to the 1960 Dragline, except a Clam Bucket and trip assembly was added. Another rare one year only set is the #146. The Low Boy Trailer was heavier and wider to accommodate the Giant Dozer. This Tonka Construction model is rare and will be difficult to add to your Tonka collection.

1956 Boxed Hi-Way Set
#B208.

Box for Accessory
Hi-Way sign set #AC300.

Accessory Hi-Way sign set
#AC300.

1959 Accessory Hi-Way sign set
#AC320.

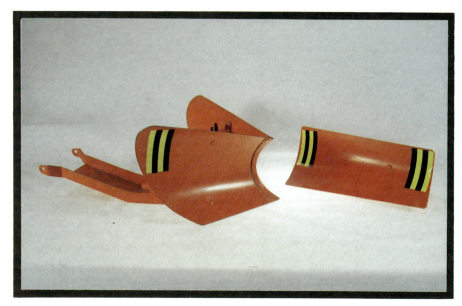

Accessory "V" Plow and Straight Plow
#AC308   #AC306.

1956 Hi-Way Pickup #02.

1956 Hi-Way Dump #20.

1956 Hi-Way Side Dump #44
(with Accessory "V" Plow).

1956 Hi-Way Grader #12
Note: Light bar behind cab.

1957 Hi-Way Pickup #02.

1957 Hi-Way Dump #20
(with Accessory "V" Plow).

1957 Hi-Way Side Dump #44.

1957 Hi-Way Grader #12.

1957 Big Mike with
Accessory "V" Plow #42.

1957 Hi-Way Low Boy
with #50 Shovel #40.

1958-59 Hi-Way Pickup.

1958-59 Hi-Way Side Dump
with Accessory "V" Plow #41.

1958-59 Hi-Way Dump
with Accessory "V" Plow.

1958 Big Mike with
Accessory "V" Plow #45.

1958 Hi-Way Low Boy and Shovel
#43.

Land Rover with box.

1959 Hydraulic Land Rover
(Rare) #42.

1960 Hi-Way Mobile Dragline #135.

1961 Hi-Way Mobile/Clam #142.

1961 Hi-Way Goose Neck Low Boy with Giant Dozer #146 (difficult to find).

1960 Tonka #100 Dozer.

1961 Giant Dozer #118.

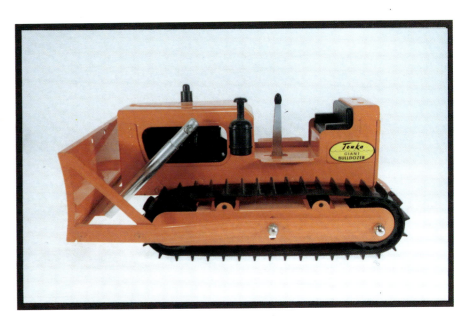

1963 Mobile Clam #942.

1960 Low Boy with Tonka #100
Dozer, 1 year only without
Hi-Way Decals #125 set.

1958 Hi-Way Low Boy with Shovel.
Only year for steam shovel – was
replaced with dragline.

1958 Hi-Way Dump with
Straight Plow from #B207 set.
Only year for front plow.

1959-60 Hi-Way Drag Line
from #B207 set.

1959-60 Hi-Way Grader #12.

1962 Spread Pack
came with #524 Dozer Packer set.

METRO VANS

The Metro Vans were produced from 1954 through 1957. Each Metro Van had a sliding door on the right side and two opening rear doors with handles. The early vans had a painted step, while vans produced in 1957 and later, had aluminum steps inside the sliding doors.

Basic vans were the #750-4 "Parcel Delivery", made in 1954 and again in 1957. The "Parcel Delivery" was produced in dark brown, and is the most frequently seen "Parcel Delivery". The more rare "Parcel Delivery" was the bronze van. In 1955, the #750-5 Carnation Milk Van was added to the Tonka line. The Carnation Van was again produced in 1956, along with a new Rescue Van. The Rescue Van was included in the Fire Sets of 1956 and 1957. There are also several private label Metro Vans known to exist. They are: G. Fox & Co., Midwest Milk, Frederick & Nelson, Marshall Field, Eibert Coffee, and Holsum Bread. Most of these were of very limited production and are very rare today.

1954 Parcel Delivery –
Metro Van #10.

1957 Parcel Delivery #10
(Bronze color unusual).

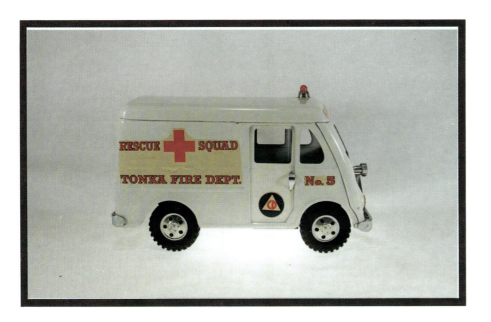

1956-57 Rescue Squad Van
(came with ladder and pumper)
B212 set.

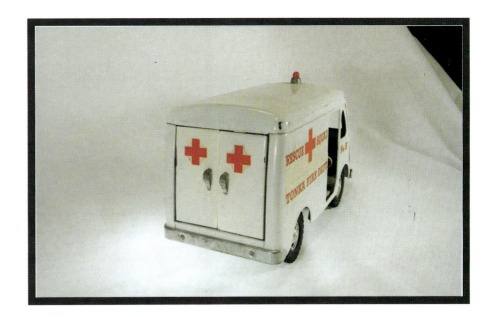

1956 Rescue Van with
red crosses on back doors.

1955 Carnation Milk Van.

1954 Eibert Coffee
Metro Van.

1954 Marshall Field & Co.
Metro Van.

1954 G. Fox & Co.
Metro Van.

1956 Holsum Bread Van.
(very rare)

Back view of 1956 Holsum Bread Van.

PICKUP TRUCKS

The first Pickup Truck manufactured by Tonka was the #880-5 "Round Fendered" Pickup made in 1955 and painted all red. The tailgate was fastened with plated tailgate chains, and the words "Tonka Toys" in slash style embossed in it, making this truck a real pleasure to collectors.

The 1956 #880-6 Pickup was painted dark blue, when sold individually, orange when purchased in the #975-6 State Hi-Way set, or red when purchased in the #875-6 Builders Supply set. Note the 1956 Hi-Way Pickup decals on the cab of this pickup carry the number 975 on them. The 1957 #02 Pickup was sold only in midnight blue or again in Omaha orange in the #B-208 State Hi-Way set. No red 1957 Pickup Trucks were produced. "Round Fendered" Pickups are very popular with collectors and command very high prices when found in excellent condition.

Tonka produced two versions of the "Square Fendered" Pickup trucks in 1958. The #02 Pickup in dark blue and the #05 Sportsman, the first of many recreational vehicles by Tonka, had a blue steel topper over the Pickup bed. Tonka changed the color of the Pickup in 1959 to tan and added white sidewalls, a new solid hubcap, and deleted the tailgate chains. In 1961, another new style Pickup was added to the Tonka line. The Fleetside or Style Side Pickup was added. Still available was the Step Side Pickup Truck. The #117 Fleetside Pickup was sold with a trailer carrying a load of stacking, plastic boats. This set was produced only once a year and is very difficult to find.

1955 Pickup #880-5.

1956 Pickup
(red only came with
interchangable bed set).

1956 Blue Pickup #02.

1957 Blue Pickup #02.

1957 Pickup with
Stake Trailer #28.

1956 State Hi-Way
Department Pickup.

1957 State Hi-Way
Department Pickup.

1959 State Hi-Way
Department Pickup.

1955 Gambles Pickup
(these pickups were made
from 1955-1963).

1960 Gambles Pickup.

Tail Gate for Gambles Pickup.

1958 Blue Pickup #02.

1958 Sportsman #05.

1958 Deluxe Sportsman with
boat and trailer #34.

1959 Deluxe Sportsman with
boat and trailer #22.

1959 Sportsman Pickup with
boat mounted on camper shell #5.

1959 Bronze Pickup with
Accessory Trailer and sheep #28.

1960 Pickup #02.

1960 Deluxe Fisherman with
Tonka Clipper #130.

1961 Red Pickup #02.

1961 Deluxe Fisherman with
Tonka Clipper #130.

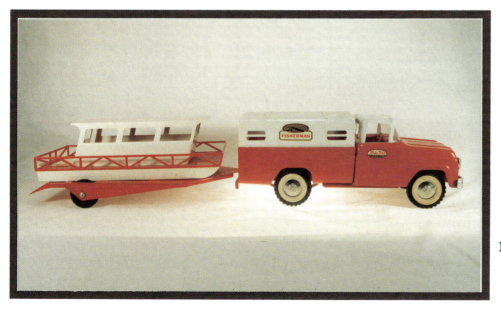

1961 Fisherman with Houseboat
(Houseboat is rare) #136.

1961 Boat Service #117.

1961 Trailer Sales Set #B206.

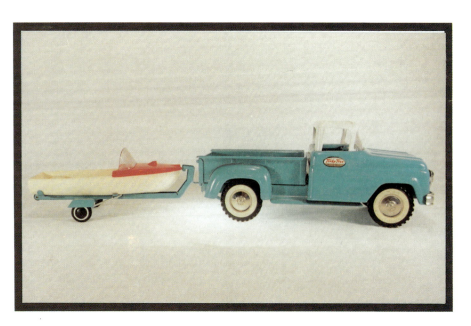

1961 Deluxe Sportsman #22

1962 Jet Delivery #410
(rare truck only made one year).

1962 Sportsman #405

1963 Generic Pickup #302

1963 Western Auto.

1963 Terminix Fleetside Pickup.
(Rare)

1963 Pickup with camper #530.

1965 Black Pickup
with Camper #530.

1966 Air Force Ambulance #402.

SEMI TRUCKS

Tonka's first semi trailer, the #140 Tonka Toy Transport, was first manufactured in 1949. This red semi with a silver roof had a slip lever latch to lock the rear doors. This latching mechanism was used on all semi doors until 1953. Also in 1949, Tonka introduced the #130 Carry-All semi or low boy.

In 1950, Tonka manufactured the #145 Steel Carrier and changed the Tonka Toy Transport by eliminating the silver roof and made it all red.

The first "Allied" Van appeared in 1951. This semi was produced as a standard Tonka product until 1981. 1952 was the introduction of the #500 Live Stock Van, and it remained basically unchanged except for decals and cab changes until 1961. 1952 also saw the first Grain Hauler, the #550.

A beautiful semi made its appearance in 1953, the #650-3 "Green Giant" transport. This was an all white semi with a reefer or refrigerator unit mounted on the front and a Green Giant holding a pea pod, largely displayed on the sides. This semi was made until 1957. The Tonka Logger was also added to the product line in 1953, and continued until 1961.

The #34 Thunderbird Express appeared in 1957. The first semi had a single axle on the rear with fixed loading gear and mud flaps. The Thunderbird in 1960 was all red and a white cab roof used the same decals.

Tonka introduced to their product line the #59 Nation Wide Moving Van in 1958. This semi replaced the "Allied" for that year and is hard to find being only a one year production truck.

1959 began the long run of car carriers with the introduction of the #40 Car Carrier. It was shipped with three 1957 Chevrolet Bel-Airs. These were plastic vehicles. The use of 1957 cars on a 1959 transporter was due to the fact that Tonka did not have molds for a toy car and had to use another toy manufacturer's molds. They were later replaced in 1960 with Ford Falcons.

Private label semi trucks have always been of interest to Tonka collectors. These were low production runs of a standard Tonka semi that contained the logo or design of a specific client. These were never listed in or sold through the catalogs of Tonka. Due to the fact no records were kept by Tonka on numbers of production or the private labels themselves, little is known about them and documentation is difficult. Because the private label trucks are highly sought after by collectors, excellent examples command premium prices today. The following is a list of private label semi trucks that are known to have been manufactured by Tonka:

Ace Hardware	Minute Maid Semi
American Breeders	Morrell Meats
Cross Country Freight	Our Own Hardware
Flavor Kist	RCD Fast Freight
Gambles	Red Owl
G. Fox & Co.	Republic Van Lines
Hormel	Rikes
Janney Semple Hill	Stix, Baer & Fuller
Jewel Tea	United Van Lines
Kroger	U.S. Air Force
Kroller Furniture	V-2000 Stores
Marshall Field & Co.	Wheaton
Meier & Frank	Yonkers

1954-55 Steel Carrier #145.

1954-57 Log Hauler #14.

1954-57 Livestock Van #36.

1955 Tonka Grain Hauler #550.

1956 Tonka Cargo King #30.

1956 Tonka Freighter.

1954 Low Boy and Shovel #120
Note: Side plates on shovel
trailer wheels below trailer.

1956 Shovel and carry-all #120.

1956 Allied Van Lines #38.

1955 Ace Hardware Semi.

1956 Gambles Semi.

1956 Morrell Meats Semi.

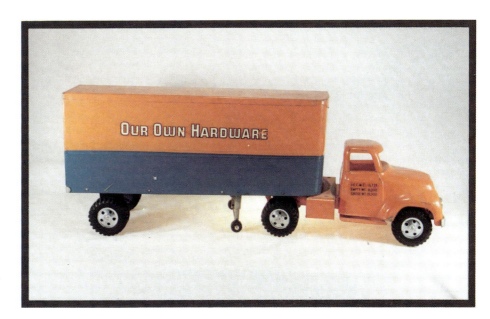

1956 Our Own Hardware Semi.

1954 Jewel Tea Company Semi.

1954 RCD Fast Freight Semi.

1954 The Rike-Kumler Co. Semi.

1955 Marshall Field and
Company Semi.

1954 Hormel Meats Semi.

1955 Minute Maid Semi.
(Rare)

1956 United Van Lines Semi.
(Rare)

1956 Wheaton Van Lines.

1955 Cross Country Freight Semi.

1957 Thunderbird Semi #34
Note: Single rear axle.

1958 Nation Wide Moving #39.
This truck replaced The Allied
Moving Van for one year only.

1959 Thunderbird Semi #37.

1959 Thunderbird Semi #37.

1960 Flavor Kist Semi.

1959 Gambles Semi.

1959 Wheaton Van Lines.

1959 Red Owl Semi.

1959 V-2000 Stores Semi.

1960 Republic Van Lines Semi.

1961 Allied Van Lines #39.

1963 Allied Van Lines.
Note: Darker orange color.

1963 Air Force Semi
(From Dayton Air Force Base).

1963 Swanson Bros. Moving Van.

1963 Stix, Baer & Fuller.
This truck was also made in 1953.

1963 Kroehler Semi.

1965 Wheaton Van Lines Semi.
Note: Closed Cab Windows.

1960 Car Hauler.
Earlier 1959 Hauler carried
a load of '57 Chevys.

1961 Car Hauler
Note: The white walls and
darker yellow.

1963 Car Carrier #840.

1959-60 Tonka Marine Service
#41.

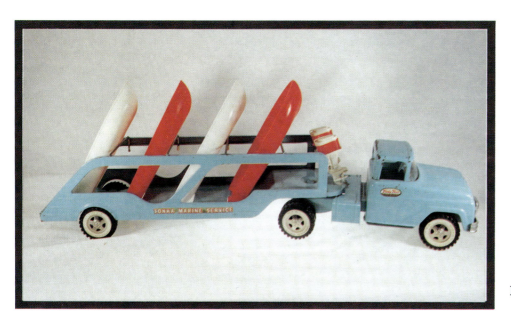

1961 Tonka Marine Service.
Light blue only in 1961 #130.

1959 Log Hauler.

1960 Single Axle Log Hauler #07.

STAKE RACK TRUCKS

Tonka introduced the first Stake Rack Truck in 1955. The #860-5 Stake Truck had an extended wheel base, four inches, was painted all red with eight, dark green removable steel stakes and mud flaps. The 850-5 Lumber Truck also had an extended frame with an aluminum bed and a load of 36 miniature pine boards, 11 7/8 inches long, 13/16 inches wide, and 1/4 inch thick, held in place by two chains, with a roller to help remove the boards. Both the Stake Bed Truck and the Lumber Bed could be removed by tripping a lever in the bottom, middle of the chassis. The long wheel base truck was packaged in a set, the #875-5 Builders Supply Fleet in 1955 and again in 1956. The set included both lumber and stake beds along with a red Pickup Truck. This was a great little set for $10.95 in its day. Also produced in 1956 and 1957 was light blue #925 Tonka Farms Truck with six dark blue stakes.

New for 1957 was the #32 Tonka Stock Rack Truck. This truck came with plastic animals as follows: brown sheep, black bull and brown horse. The extended cab and chassis were painted dark blue and the racks were red. The rear rack would slide up and down. The B202 Tonka Stock Farm was produced in 1957. This set contained the #04 Stock Rack Truck, six animals, a wood corral, and an aluminum loading ramp. A very rare unique truck manufactured in 1957 was the #22 Lumber Truck. This truck was an extended chassis truck with a permanently fixed aluminum bed carrying 36 boards and only one chain. There are not many of this particular truck around. Tonka produced three rack bodied trucks in 1958; the #04 Tonka Farms short wheel base truck now in emerald green with white racks, the #32 High Rack or Stock Rack Truck in all white cab and chassis with red racks, and the #03 utility truck. The utility truck had a long wheel base and the aluminum lumber bed permanently fixed to it. No roller for the lumber was used. In 1959 Tonka eliminated the aluminum bed and made one of stamped steel calling it the #03 Platform Stake Truck. Painted in bright yellow, this long wheel base truck was manufactured only one year and is quite rare.

Another interesting truck manufactured by Tonka in 1959 was the #30 Tandem Stake Truck. Identical to the #30 Platform Stake Truck, the bronze truck and trailer, which was identical to the bed used on the truck, had steerable front wheels and a hitch. The trailer also had dual wheels front and rear and white sidewalls were added. Made only in 1959, the Tandem Stake Truck is a great addition to any Tonka collection.

1955 Lumber Truck #0850-5.

1955 Stake Truck #0860-5.

1956 Stake Truck.

1956 Lumber Truck with original load and chains.

1955-56 Lumber Load came with small red flag attached to wood.

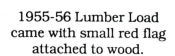

1957 Lumber Truck #22.
(rare bronze color)

1958 Platform Stake Truck
or Utility Truck #03.

1959 Tandem Platform
Stake Truck #30.

1959 Platform Stake Truck #03.
(Rare yellow color)

1957 Stock Rack Farm Truck #32.

1958 Tonka Farms Stock Rack #32.

1959 Stock Rack Farm Truck #32.

1956 Tonka Farms Rack Truck #04.

1957 Tonka Farms Rack Truck #04.

1958 Tonka Farms Stake Truck #04.

1959 Tonka Farms Stake Truck #04.

1959 Tonka Farms with
Horse Trailer #35.

1961 Farm Set #B204.

1959 Ferry Brothers.

1961 Green Giant Rack Truck.

1961 Doughboy Feeds.

1963 Rack Truck Generic #404.

1962 Generic Farm
Stake Rack Pickup #308.

1964 Generic Farm Stake
Rack Truck #308.

1965 Stake Rack Pickup #504.

TANKER TRUCKS

Tonka made another classic truck in the Tonka Toys truck line of 1957, the #16 Gasoline Truck. Tonka made the #33 Gasoline Truck again in 1958 and a white "T – F – D" Tanker, that was only available as part of the 1958 fire set. These Tankers are very desirable and highly sought after by Tonka collectors.

In 1960 and 1961, Tonka brought back the tanker, only this time it was a semi and the tanks were made of a hard plastic. The new Tankers carried the decal, "Tonka Tanker". This Tanker was sold separately or with two bulk storage tanks and a reducer for the garden hose.

A rare variation was made of these Semi Tankers. A "Standard" decal replaced the usual "Tonka Tanker" decal and was available in 1960. A modified "Standard" was produced in 1961. The "Standard" gas logo had a white background covering the entire length of the tank. These are rare trucks, and make excellent additions to the Tonka Gas Truck collection.

1957 Gasoline Tanker #16.

1958 Gasoline Tanker #33.

1958 T.F.D. Tanker
comes with #58 Fire Set.

1960-61 Tonka Tanker #145.

1961 Standard Tanker.

1961 Standard Tanker.

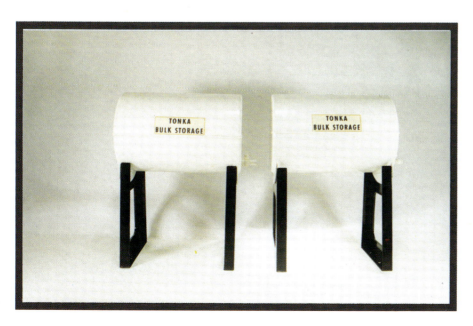

1960-61 Bulk Storage Tanks
came with Tonka Tanker set.

1961 Bulk Storage Set #B215.

1957 Gas Truck
shown with its box.

1958 Gasoline Truck
has "HOSE" on back door.

UTILITY TRUCKS

Tonka first introduced the Utility Truck in 1950. The #175 Utility was a cabover truck with a green cab and chassis, and a yellow stamped steel stake body. There is no end gate on this truck, however a chain was attached across the rear of the stake box. The #175 Utility Hauler colors were changed in 1952. The cab and chassis were orange and the utility bed was green. In 1954, the Green Giant Company requested that Tonka make a special promotional toy. Tonka used the 1953 Utility Truck, painted it white, and placed a Green Giant Company decal on the cab, and a Green Giant Peas decal with the Jolly Green Giant on the side of the utility box. The tires were the new all rubber design on a cabover truck, the only cabover with new style tires. Approximately 5,000 of the cabover Green Giant Promotional utility trucks were produced.

Finding a nice one for your collection will be difficult. A very rare utility, is the 1954 "Round Fendered" Green Giant Utility, identical to the cabover version that was a special promotional toy for the Green Giant Company. No production figures are known for this truck. However, there are far less "Round Fendered" Green Giant Utility Trucks than the cabover version. "Round Fendered" utility trucks were manufactured in 1954, the #175-4 Utility Truck had an orange cab and chassis with a green utility bed. Although the Utility Truck was dropped in 1955, a number of promotional or private label models were produced. The Star-Kist Utility with green cab and chassis and white bed, was made in two versions, one with plain white bed, and one with cans of tuna depicted on the sides of the bed. Another unusual special utility was the Our Own Hardware. This truck had a blue cab and chassis, and orange bed, and Our Own Hardware logo on the side of the bed. Any of these Utility Trucks would make an excellent addition to your Tonka collection.

Utility Truck
1950-51 Green Cab / Yellow Body.
1952-53 Orange Cab / Green Body.

1952 Coast to Coast
Utility Truck.

Green Giant Utility 1953 cabover
solid rubber tires as used
in later years.

1954 Utility Truck #175.

1954 Green Giant Utility Truck
#175.

1954 Star-Kist Utility Truck
with cans on sides.

1955 Star-Kist Utility Truck.

1957 Our Own Hardware
Utility Truck.

WRECKER TRUCKS

The Wrecker Truck first appeared in the Tonka product line in 1949. The #250 Wrecker Truck carried the MM (Mound Minnesota) logo on its side. This all blue truck with a red boom was made from 1949-1953. It was then replaced by the all new red and white "Round Fender" Tow Truck of 1954. The "Round Fender" Wrecker Trucks were made from 1954-1957. The 1954-1955 Wrecker Trucks had a red cab and white body, while the 1956-1957 Tow Trucks were all white. Scarce and collectible, is the #960-6 AAA Wrecker Truck, an all white Wrecker produced in 1956. Tonka made this truck for about six months, and replaced it with the AA logo. A licensing dispute between Tonka and AAA ended its production almost as quickly as it began.

The "Square Fender" Trucks of 1958-1961 show Wrecker Trucks well represented as each year a Wrecker Truck was available. A highly desirable Wrecker Truck of this era is the rare 1961 Standard Tow Truck. This truck is visually attractive because of its red color and standard logos. Keep looking, they're out there.

1953 Cabover Wrecker Truck #250.

1954 Wrecker Truck.

1955 Wrecker Truck.

1956 Wrecker Truck.

1956 AAA Wrecker Truck
Black Boom.

1956 AAA Wrecker Truck
Red Boom.

1957 Wrecker Truck
(AA) #18.

1958-61 Wrecker Truck #18.

1961 Standard Wrecker Truck.
(Rare)

1963 Generic Wrecker Truck #518.

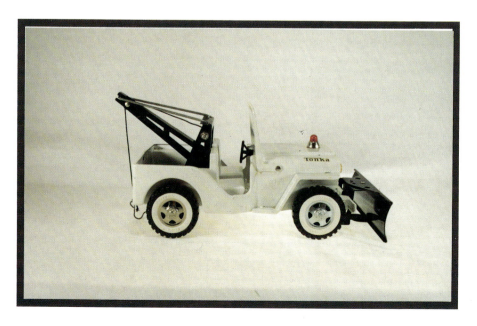

1964 Jeep Wrecker #375.

MISCELLANEOUS TRUCKS
AND ACCESSORIES

These groupings of Tonka Toys are products that would not fit into the previous chapters in this book. Many are very unique and very limited in production. One truck in particular is the #115 metallic blue with an aluminum boom. The purpose of the boom was to lift logs. This truck was also packaged in set #B-201, the Timber Company. This set included the power boom, logger truck with a load of four logs, and beams held by chains.

Another truck manufactured by Tonka was the #120 Cement mixer. First appearing in 1960 as the black walled variety, the cement mixer was made for many years to come by Tonka.

1962 and 1963 the #201 Ser-Vi-Car appeared. This three wheeled trike was white. The only difference between the two cars is a minor decal change.

The #101 Golf Club Tractor and the #301 Utility dump manufactured in 1961 - 1962 respectively, are very unique and limited production run items. They make excellent additions to your Tonka collections.

Another unique Tonka toy for 1962 was the #420 Tractor and Luggage Trailer. Each trailer had five plastic suitcases. 1963 saw a very unique and desirable truck, the #640 Ramp Hoist. The ramp hoist was red with a white roof. A even rarer version is the 1964 green ramp hoist. Keep looking, they are out there.

1960 Cement Truck #120.

1963 Cement Truck #620.

108

1960 Power Boom Loader #115.
(Rare)

1959 Sanitary Service Truck.
Truck came with two bins and
one scoop #B203.

1960 Sanitary Service Truck #140.

1961 Sanitary Service Truck #140
Note: White walls and bumpers).
(Rare)

1961 Golf Club Tractor #101.

1962 Utility Dump #301.

1963 Ramp Hoist #640.

1964 Ramp Hoist
(rare green color) #640.

Left: 1963   Right: 1962
Servi Car both variations.

1962 Tonka Airport Service
#2100.

1963 Tonka Air Lines.

1963 Tractor. This also came in
yellow, blue, and red, #250.

1963 Back Hoe #422.

1964 Tonka Jeep with
Tonka Clipper #516.

1956-57 Accessory Scraper Blade
with box.

Corral with Animals #AC316

1957-59 Accessory Corral
with Animals #AC316.

1957 Box Trailer #AC310.

1957 Accessory Stake Trailer
with box #AC312.

1957 Accessory Boat
and Motor #AC311.

1960 Tonka Clipper #AC360.

1958 Red Stake Trailer with Sheep.
1960 Stake Trailer #AC312.

1959-60 Box Trailer #AC310.
1958-61 Tonka Farms
Horse Trailer #AC311.

1959 Dragline, unique in color.
Only sold in set #B205 Dragline &
Crane Set. (Came with single axle log
hauler and dump truck.)

1964 Army Tractor #250.

1964 Army Troop Carrier #380.

1964 Giant Army Dozer #536.

1964 Army Jeep & Trailer #384.

1963 Trencher #534

1964 Shovel #526

118

1966 Bulldozer #300.

1963 Gold plated Mini-Tonka Pickup.

These were presented to major distributors, or wholesalers. Only eighty were passed out. (Very Rare)
(quite a find for your collection.)

1979 Customer Performance Award.

Made in 24 gauge stainless steel limited to 100 trucks, given to outstanding retailers.

1980 A.J. Foyt Indy Race Team
#2004.

Georgia Power Pickup.

Georgia Power Bucket Truck.

Keep your boxes! They could add 20-50% to the
value of a Tonka Truck!

TONKA SETS 1953-1963

1953

#675 "Tonka" Trailer Fleet Set.
Contains: 1-red cab, 1-blue cab, carry-all trailer, grain hauler trailer, livestock van, log trailer, and steel carrier.

1954

#675-4 "Tonka" Trailer Fleet Set.
Contains: 1-red cab, 1-orange cab, steel carrier, log trailer, livestock van, grain hauler.

#775-4 Road Builder Set.
Contains: Grader, dump truck, low boy and steam shovel.

1955

#675-5 "Tonka" Trailer Fleet Set.
Contains: 2-red cabs, grain hauler, livestock van, logger, steel carrier.

#775-5 Road Builder Set.
Contains: Dump truck, shovel and carry-all, road grader.

#825-5 Aerial Sandloader Set.
Contains: Dump truck, aerial sandloader.

#875-5 Builders Supply Fleet Set.
Contains: Lumber truck with load, pickup, stake truck bed.

1956

#675-6 "Tonka" Trailer Fleet Set.
Contains: 2-cabs, Cargo King trailer, log trailer, livestock van, Tonka freight trailer.

#775-6 Road Builder Set.
Contains: Dump truck, shovel and carry-all, road grader.

#825-6 Aerial Sand Loader Set.
Contains: Dump truck, aerial sand loader.

#875-6 Builders Supply Fleet Set.
Contains: Lumber truck with load, pickup (red), stake truck bed.

#900-6 Tonka Fire Department.
Contains: Suburban pumper, aerial ladder, special rescue squad van, fire chief badge.

#975-6 State Hi-Way Department Set (orange).
Contains: Dump truck, hydraulic side dump, pickup, road grader, set of eight road signs.

1957

#B200 "Tonka" Trailer Rental Set.
Contains: Pickup, two box trailers, one stake trailer.

#B202 "Tonka" Stock Farm.
Contains: Farm stake truck, wood corral, six plastic animals.

#B204 Tonka Truck – Trailer Rental
Contains: Pickup, stake truck, box trailer, stake trailer.

#B206 "Tonka" Trailer Fleet Set.
Contains: 2-cabs, Tonka logger, Tonka "Cargo King", livestock van, and four animals.

#B208 State Hi-Way Department Set (orange).
Contains: Pickup, dump truck, side dump, grader and eight hi-way signs.

#B210 Road Builder Set.
Contains: Big Mike with plow, low boy and shovel, grader, dump truck.

#B212 "Tonka Fire Department.
Contains: Suburban pumper, aerial ladder, rescue squad van, fire chief badge.

1958

#B202 Tonka Farm Set.
Contains: Stock rack truck, wood corral, six animals.

#B204 Truck Trailer Rental.
Contains: Pickup, farm stake truck, stake trailer, box trailer.

#B205 Farm Set.
Contains: Stock rack, farm stake truck, stake trailer, horse trailer.

#B207 Hi-Way Construction Set (lime green)
Contains: Dump truck with scraper blade, road grader, steam shovel, carry-all trailer.

#B209 Deluxe Farm Set.
Contains: Livestock van, farm stake truck, stock rack, horse trailer, corral and animals.

#B211 State Hi-Way Department (orange)
Contains: Dump truck with scraper blade, hydraulic dump with snow plow, pickup, grader, eight road signs.

#B213 Fire Department.
Contains: Tanker truck, suburban pumper, aerial ladder.

1959

#B202 Stock Farm Set.
Contains: Stock rack truck, corral and four animals.

#B203 Sanitary Service Set.

Contains: Sanitary truck, two refuse containers, one scoop.

#B204 Farm Set.
Contains: Farm stake truck, pickup, horse trailer, stake trailer and four animals.

#B205 Dragline and Crain Set.
Contains: Dump truck, dragline, single axle logger.

#B206 Trailer Sales Set.
Contains: Sportsman, pickup, box trailer, horse trailer, boat trailer.

#B207 Hi-Way Construction Set (lime green).
Contains: dump truck, equipment trailer, drag line, road grader.

#B210 State Hi-Way Department Set (orange).
Contains: Dump truck, hydraulic side dump, pickup, grader, eight road signs.

#B212 Fire Department Set (white).
Contains: Suburban pumper, aerial ladder, fire chief badge.

1960

#B200 Stock Farm Set.
Contains: Farm Stake Truck, wood corral, 4-animals, stake trailer.

#B201 Timber Company.
Contains: Power boom loader, timber truck, 4-logs and 4-beams.

#B204 Farm Set.
Contains: Pickup, farm stake truck, stake trailer, horse trailer.

#B206 Trailer Sales Set.
Contains: Pickup, sportsman with boat, box trailer, stake trailer, horse trailer, boat's trailer.

#B207 Hi-Way Construction Set (lime green).
Contains: Dump truck, road grader, dragline, equipment trailer.

#B215 Bulk Storage Set.
Contains: Tanker truck, 2-storage tanks.

#B218 Paving Department Set.
Contains: Dump truck, #100 Dozer, cement truck, road grader, 2-signs (slow & stop).

#B220 State Turnpike Set (orange)
Contains: Dump truck, pickup, mobile dragline, #100 dozer with 3-signs (slow, stop, caution barrier).

#B225 Fire Department Set.
Contains: Suburban pumper, aerial ladder, rescue squad truck with boat strapped to top, fire chief badge.

1961

#B202 Country Club Service Set.

Contains: Golf club tractor, pickup, dozer and trailer.

#B204 Farm Set.
Contains: Pickup, farm stake, horse trailer, stake trailer with animals.

#B206 Trailer Sales Set.
Contains: Pickup, sportsman, horse trailer, stake trailer, box trailer, boat and trailer.

#B215 Bulk Storage Set.
Contains: Two storage tanks, Tonka Tanker.

#B216 Road Builders Set.
Contains: Grader, dump truck, sand loader, dozer and trailer.

#B218 Paving Department Set.
Contains: Grader, dump truck, cement truck, dozer.

#B219 Construction Set.
Contains: Dump truck, mobile clam, giant dozer.

1962

#2100 Airport Service Set.
Contains: Tractor with two trailers, ten suitcases, jeep, ser-vi-car.

#2110 Marina.
Contains: Pickup, house boat, speedboat on trailer, motorboat on trailer.

#2120 Farm Set.
Contains: Farm stake, pickup, stake trailer, horse trailer, and three animals.

#2130 Super Service Set.
Contains: Wrecker, jeep, ser-vi-car, stake trailer, and box trailer.

#2150 Road Builder Set.
Contains: Grader, dump truck, sand loader, dozer, and trailer.

#2190 Construction Set.
Contains: Cement mixer, dump truck, bulldozer, eleven wheel spread pack, dozer loader.

1963

#2100 Airport Service Set.
Contains: Tractor with two trailers, ten suitcases, jeep, ser-vi-car.

#2120 Farm Set.
Contains: Farm stake, pickup, stake trailer, horse trailer, three animals.

#2140 Outdoor Living Set.
Contains: Jeep surry, jeep run about with four suitcases, Tonka clipper, camper.

#2160 Contractor Set.
Contains: Dump truck, grader, sand loader, trencher.

TONKA ACCESSORIES

Tonka accessories first appeared in 1957. They were intended to increase the play value of their related vehicles. Accessory sets were available through 1960.

1957

#AC-306	Scraper blade with mounting bracket
#AC-312	Stake trailer
#AC-300	Hi-Way sign set
#AC-304	Tonka farm animals
#AC-310	Tonka box trailer
#AC-308	"V" blade snow plow with mounting bracket

1958

#AC-310	Box trailer
#AC-311	Boat, motor, and trailer
#AC-312	Stake trailer
#AC-314	Horse trailer and two horses
#AC-316	Corral and four animals
#AC-318	Snow plow, scraper blade with bracket
#AC-320	Hi-Way sign set

1959

#AC-300	Scale model cars – three 1957 Chevrolet cars
#AC-310	Box trailers
#AC-311	Boat, trailer and motor
#AC-312	Stake trailer
#AC-314	Horse trailer and two horses
#AC-316	Corral and animals
#AC-318	Scraper blade snow plow and bracket
#AC-320	Hi-Way sign set

1960

	Marine Accessories
#AC-345	Deluxe boat
#AC-350	Deluxe boat and trailer
#AC-360	Tonka clipper
#AC-370	Tonka clipper and trailer
	Accessories
#AC-308	Three scale autos
#AC-310	Box trailer
#AC-312	Stake trailer
#AC-314	Horse trailer
#AC-316	Corral and four animals
#AC-318	Scraper blade and bracket
#AC-319	Snow plow and bracket
#AC-320	Hi-Way sign set
#AC-325	Assorted plastic animals
#AC-330	The falcon

Price Guide

The current prices in this book should be used only as a guide. They are not to set prices, which vary from one section of the country to another. Dealers prices vary greatly and are affected by condition as well as demand. Neither the Author nor the Publisher assumes responsibility for any losses or gains that might be a result of consulting this guide.

(Prices are: **Good   Excellent   Mint**)

PAGE 13
$125 225 425

PAGE 14
Top: $ 90 125 200
Middle: 90 125 200
Bottom: 90 125 200

PAGE 15
Top: $150 275 500
Bottom: 90 125 200

PAGE 16
Top: $ 90 125 200
Middle: 90 125 200
Bottom: 50 75 125

PAGE 17
Top: $100 175 300
Middle: 90 150 250
Bottom: 125 325 550

PAGE 18
Top: $125 185 300
Middle: 100 175 250
Bottom: 100 175 250

PAGE 19
Top: $125 185 300
Middle: 75 150 250
Bottom: 75 150 250

PAGE 20
Top: $100 150 225
Middle: 125 175 250
Bottom: 125 175 225

PAGE 21
Top: $125 175 250
Middle: 150 225 375
Bottom: 150 225 350

PAGE 22
Top: $150 225 375
Middle: 150 225 375
Bottom: 150 225 375

PAGE 23
Top: $200 350 600
Middle: 200 350 600
Bottom: 200 350 600

PAGE 24
Top: $200 350 675
Middle: 200 375 500
Middle: 200 375 500
Bottom: 300 500 750

PAGE 26
Top: $125 325 550
Bottom: 175 375 650

PAGE 27
Top: $175 375 650
Middle: 175 375 650
Bottom: 250 475 750

PAGE 28
Top: $250 375 650
Middle: 250 450 800
Bottom: 200 350 650

PAGE 29
Top: $250 400 750
Middle: 250 400 750
Middle: 125 200 375
Bottom: 175 300 475

PAGE 30
Top: $ 75 125 250
Middle: 75 150 275
Bottom: 100 175 325

PAGE 32
Top: $ 90 160 275
Middle: 175 275 450
Bottom: 175 275 450

PAGE 33
Top: $ 75 150 225
Middle: 75 160 250
Bottom: 95 150 250

PAGE 34
Top: $100 175 300
Middle: 300 500 850
Bottom: 100 175 300

PAGE 35
Top: $125 225 350
Middle: 300 500 850
Bottom: 450 600 950

PAGE 36
Top: $ 65 100 150
Middle: 65 100 175
Bottom: 95 175 250

PAGE 37
Top: $ 65 100 175
Middle: 100 175 275
Middle: 100 150 225
Bottom: 50 95 150

PAGE 38
Top: $125 250 400
Bottom: 125 225 375

PAGE 39
Top: $125 275 375
Middle: 100 175 275

Bottom: 200 350 550

PAGE 40
Top: $100 150 225
Middle: 100 225 350
Bottom: 300 450 750

PAGE 41
Top: $100 250 350
Middle: 100 250 350
Bottom: 100 175 275

PAGE 42
Top: $100 250 400
Middle: 75 150 225
Bottom: 75 150 225

PAGE 43
Top: $100 200 325
Bottom: 95 175 300

PAGE 44
$600 900 1500

PAGE 45
Top: $125 200 300
Middle: 125 200 300
Bottom: 125 200 300

PAGE 46
Top: $ 75 175 275
Middle: 100 200 300
Bottom: 95 150 250

PAGE 47
Top: $100 250 400
Middle: 75 150 200
Bottom: 100 200 300

PAGE 48
Top: $100 225 350
Middle: 100 200 300
Bottom: 75 125 175

PAGE 49
Top: $300 500 850
Middle: 175 300 450
Bottom: 75 150 225

PAGE 50
Top: $125 225 350
Middle: 125 200 300
Bottom: 300 500 850

PAGE 51
Top: $175 250 375
Middle: 600 900 1200
Bottom: 450 600 950

PAGE 52
Top: $100 200 300

Middle: 100 200 300
Bottom: 200 350 550

PAGE 53
Top: $ 50 75 175
Middle: 75 150 275
Bottom: 100 185 250

PAGE 54
Top: $100 175 275
Middle: 125 225 325
Bottom: 95 150 250

PAGE 55
Top: $100 175 250
Middle: 75 100 175
Bottom: 100 175 250

PAGE 56
Top: $100 225 375
Bottom: 125 250 400

PAGE 57
Top: $100 225 350
Middle: 100 225 350
Bottom: 100 225 350

PAGE 58
Top: $175 300 550
Middle: 150 300 550
Bottom: 175 375 600

PAGE 59
Top: $300 500 850
Bottom: 300 500 850

PAGE 60
$100 200 300

PAGE 61
Top: $150 275 450
Middle: 100 200 300
Bottom: 100 200 300

PAGE 62
Top: $175 275 375
Middle: 100 200 300
Bottom: 100 200 300

PAGE 63
Top: $ 75 150 225
Middle: 125 225 350
Bottom: 100 150 225

PAGE 64
Top, just a view of the tail gate
Middle: $ 75 125 200
Bottom: 100 175 250

PAGE 65
Top: $125 225 350
Middle: 100 175 250

Bottom: 75 150 225

PAGE 66
Top: $100 150 225
Middle: 75 125 200
Bottom: 150 250 350

PAGE 67
Top: $ 75 125 200
Middle: 150 250 350
Bottom: 175 275 400

PAGE 68
Top: $150 250 350
Middle: 250 350 550
Bottom: 100 175 250

PAGE 69
Top: $125 275 450
Middle: 75 150 250
Bottom: 65 150 180

PAGE 70
Top: $ 75 125 200
Middle: 200 300 500
Bottom: 75 175 275

PAGE 71
Top: $ 75 175 275
Bottom: 75 175 225

PAGE 73
Top: $100 200 275
Bottom: 75 175 250

PAGE 74
Top: $ 75 175 250
Middle: 75 175 250
Bottom: 75 175 250

PAGE 75
Top: $ 75 175 250
Middle: 100 250 375
Bottom: 100 250 375

PAGE 76
Top: $100 250 375
Middle: 275 450 800
Bottom: 150 250 425

PAGE 77
Top: $200 450 800
Middle: 175 275 450
Bottom: 200 450 800

PAGE 78
Top: $250 450 800
Middle: 250 450 800
Bottom: 250 350 650

PAGE 79
Top: $250 450 800
Middle: 700 1500 2800
Bottom: 600 1100 1800

PAGE 80
Top: $250 475 800
Middle: 175 300 450
Bottom: 150 250 375

PAGE 81
Top: $175 350 550

Middle: 150 250 400
Bottom: 150 250 375

PAGE 82
Top: $250 500 800
Middle: 100 200 300
Bottom: 175 350 500

PAGE 83
Top: $150 275 450
Middle: 275 500 900
Bottom: 350 650 1100

PAGE 84
Top: $ 75 175 300
Middle: 75 175 300
Bottom: 175 300 500

PAGE 85
Top: $250 400 700
Middle: 250 400 700
Bottom: 250 425 775

PAGE 86
Top: $175 350 550
Middle: 100 200 325
Bottom: 100 200 325

PAGE 87
Top: $100 175 275
Middle: 100 250 450
Bottom: 100 275 500

PAGE 88
Top: $ 75 150 225
Bottom: 75 150 250

PAGE 89
$125 225 375

PAGE 90
Top: $125 225 375
Middle: 125 225 375
Middle: 125 250 375
Bottom is back view of above

PAGE 91
Top: $175 250 450
Middle: 125 200 350
Bottom: 175 275 450

PAGE 92
Top: $175 300 500
Middle: 175 275 450
Bottom: 160 250 400

PAGE 93
Top: $150 250 400
Middle: 100 200 300
Bottom: 100 200 300

PAGE 94
Top: $ 75 150 250
Middle: 75 150 250
Bottom: 75 175 350

PAGE 95
Top: $250 375 550
Middle: 150 250 400
Middle: 150 250 350
Bottom: 150 275 400

PAGE 96
Top: $100 175 250
Middle: 75 150 200
Middle: 75 150 200
Bottom: 75 125 200

PAGE 97
$300 500 800

PAGE 98
Top: $300 400 700
Middle: 300 450 750
Bottom: 150 275 400

PAGE 99
Top: $250 450 675
Middle: 250 500 850
Bottom: 100 200 300

PAGE 100
Top: $300 550 800
Middle: 500 800 1200
Bottom is back view of above

PAGE 101
Top: $100 175 250
Bottom: 125 185 300

PAGE 102
Top: $100 185 300
Middle: 100 185 275
Bottom: 100 200 350

PAGE 103
Top: $100 200 375
Middle: 100 200 350
Bottom: 100 225 400

PAGE 104
Top: $100 175 300
Bottom: 100 175 325

PAGE 105
Top: $100 175 325
Middle: 100 200 350
Bottom: 175 275 500

PAGE 106
Top: $175 275 500
Middle: 100 200 300
Bottom: 75 125 250

PAGE 107
Top: $200 350 600
Middle: 50 100 200
Bottom: 50 100 175

PAGE 108
Top: $100 185 300
Bottom: 100 175 275

PAGE 109
Top: $175 350 600
Middle: 200 400 700
Bottom: 175 325 575

PAGE 110
Top: $200 400 700
Middle: 75 150 225
Bottom: 75 150 225

PAGE 111
Top: $175 300 500
Middle: 250 450 750
Bottom: 50 125 200

PAGE 112
Top: $100 150 200
Middle: 150 250 375
Bottom: 50 100 155

PAGE 113
Top: $ 75 175 275
Middle: 100 175 275
Bottom: 30 75 150

PAGE 114
Top: $100 150 200
Middle: 100 150 200
Bottom: 35 75 150

PAGE 115
Top: $ 35 75 150
Middle: 75 150 200
Bottom: 75 150 275

PAGE 116
Top: $ 35 65 95
Middle: 35 75 125
Bottom: 100 150 275

PAGE 117
Top: $ 50 75 150
Middle: 60 125 200
Bottom: 75 150 200

PAGE 118
Top: $ 70 100 200
Middle: 35 75 100
Bottom: 35 75 100

PAGE 119
Top: $ 35 75 100
Middle: 1000
Bottom: 500

PAGE 120
Top: $ 55 125 225
Middle: 35 75 150
Bottom: 65 150 250